THAT'S JUST THE WAY IT IS

poems by

Karen Wolf

Finishing Line Press
Georgetown, Kentucky

THAT'S JUST THE WAY IT IS

I dedicate this book to my soul mate, Chris Werkman, who convinced me to send out my poetry for publication and guided me through the mystifying computer jungle standing between me and successful submissions.

I also want to thank Shaindel Beers, my writing coach from AllWriters' Workplace & Workshop. She enabled me to turn my ideas into poetry with her encouragingly frank instruction. Lastly, I wish to thank Leah Maines, Publisher of Finishing Line Press, for believing in my work.

Copyright © 2018 by Karen Wolf
ISBN 978-1-63534-468-4 First Edition
All rights reserved under International and Pan-American Copyright Conventions. No part of this book may be reproduced in any manner whatsoever without written permission from the publisher, except in the case of brief quotations embodied in critical articles and reviews.

ACKNOWLEDGMENTS

Grateful acknowledgment is made to the journals and anthologies in which these poems first appeared:

Smoky Blue Literary and Arts Magazine: "Control"
Dime Show Review: "Fog Running"
Tree House: An Exhibition of the Arts: "Skipping Summer", and "Spider People"
The Wagon Magazine: "Just The Way It Is", "The Photo", "Flag R And R", "Held in Memory By No One", and "Losing My Religion"
Prizm, Art-A-Fair, E.E. Cumings Free Verse Award: "Don't Start the Music" and *Creative Challenge Award*: "Documentary: Rock Perceptions"
Oasis Journal 2016: "Echo Memories"
Artificium: The Journal: "Who?"
Foliate Oak Literary Magazine: "Plot Twist".
Lit.Cat: "Escape"
Sobotka Literary Magazine: "Motherhood"
The Bookends Review: "Life without Parole", and "Coping With Headlines"
The Drunken Llama: "New Paths"
Blynkt: "I Made It Out"
Communicators League: "All The World's a Stage", "Releasing the Sadness", "Execution Twice Stayed"
The Borfski Press: "Ruth"
Ground Fresh Thursday Press: "Moon Meditation"

Publisher: Leah Maines
Editor: Christen Kincaid
Cover Art: Christopher Werkman
Author Photo: Charea Jennings
Cover Design: Elizabeth Maines McCleavy

Printed in the USA on acid-free paper.
Order online: www.finishinglinepress.com
also available on amazon.com

Author inquiries and mail orders:
Finishing Line Press
P. O. Box 1626
Georgetown, Kentucky 40324
U. S. A.

Table of Contents

Control	1
Releasing The Sadness	3
Execution Twice Stayed	4
Don't Start The Music	5
Coping With Headlines	6
Spider People	7
Motherhood	8
Losing My Religion	10
Life Without Parole	11
Flag R and R	12
Fog Running	13
Echo Memories	14
Documentary: Rock Perceptions	16
Escape	18
Just The Way It Is	19
Plot Twist	21
New Paths	22
Who	23
The Photo	24
Less Worry	25
Held In Memory By No One	26
Skipping Summer	27
I Made It Out	28
Fading Fire	29
All The World's A Stage	30
Managing Rhythms	31
Moon Meditation	32
One	33
Cultural Fabric	34
Ruth	35

CONTROL

A dirty hat hides her blonde locks,
baggy clothes her enticing body.
Melon-size breasts, just like her
grandmother's, barely detectable.
They were her wild cards,
arranged in tight lacy blouses,
presented to garner a raise, a
promotion, reprieve from a traffic
ticket, a night out on the town.
Now every night is out on the town,
worldly possessions slung over her
shoulder in a plastic bag.

Her name, Mary Etta, shared
with her grandmother, once
took center stage on her business
cards, flowed in whispers
from lovers' lips, was called out,
encouraging her to push her
son into the world.
She goes by Hank now.

Sometimes trust peeks out
like a curl from beneath her hat.
She cozies up to a vet,
knowing when a plane flies over,
changing his world into a war zone,
his punches will hurt less than
being gang raped.
She's in his unit,
a member of the brotherhood,
never to be left bleeding on the field,
At least for this moment.

Security comes in fits and
starts like her sleep pattern.
Bedding down near a well-lighted
building keeps the crazies at bay.
And a planned step
across the line of sanity
provides solitude from those
longing for sexual intimacy.

Nothing is for certain
on the street, but
she has control, something
she will never relinquish to the
four walls of a shelter.

RELEASING THE SADNESS

Her mind is a tin box storing snapshots,
it sheds rust building up on her soul
like a can left out in the rain.
Piles of numbing photos gleaned from
daily life and social outlets, ever present—
handcuffs, bloodied cheek, hospital wrist band,
protruding ribs of hunger, caged animals, tornado flattened village.
Unconnected images mix with those of mouths
remaining closed in uncaring silence,
or open spewing hateful comments,
eyes that look away or never even notice.

Each photo imprints sadness, rusted layer upon layer.
Her reactions hidden behind a fake smile of normalcy
until the weight of them spills out when she sees
a vole, dead mid-trail, leaf on its head like a tiny hat.
She cries for the vole, the raptor that dropped his meal,
and the pain pulsing from every photo.
She releases his spirit and her accumulated sadness.
His delicate wholeness gives her strength to carry on.

EXECUTION TWICE STAYED
J.D. Scott (1953 – 2001)

Twice I touched the shroud of death.
Its gauzy darkness:
      dulled the taste of my final meals,
      choked back my family's good-bye words,
      jellied my muscles for the final walks.
Strapped down and pierced by needles,
my spirit struggled to embrace life.
The shroud loomed ever closer, then
vanished with each reprieving
phone call, to reaffirm the
sanctity of my life:
      a lesson learned too late for my victims,
      knowledge still unfamiliar to my government.
Surely, the third time that
shroud will wrap and wrestle me
into the darkness of my grave.

DON'T START THE MUSIC

She hated to bother
him, her, them
as they lived their
musical chair lives.
Whenever she approached,
the music stopped
and she was odd woman out,
then she backpedaled to the wall
feeling cold plaster against her palms
watching their lives bump into each other
until the unbreathable air
was thick with their
back biting, possession bragging,
and selfish posturing.
Hand over hand
she eased along the wall
and out the door
into a fresh breeze which
enabled her to:
    inhale,
    speak to birds, insects, chipmunks, and squirrels,
    to clear her mind,
    and never, ever
    start the music.

COPING WITH HEADLINES

My morning run GoFunds my soul.
A nighthawk calls from a roadside bush
quieting my muddled brain.
An owl hoots from a distant woods
drawing me into the present, in time to spot
a deer emerging from a cornfield,
a rabbit racing down the side of the road.
Fog settles in, providing inner calm.
Physically spent, spiritually rejuvenated,
I can now try to face the morning newspaper so that
the confluence of headlines becomes palatable.
        U.S. to spend 1.8 billion on nukes
        Experts offer tips on avoiding injuries
            while conducting your fall clean-up
        9,000 Syrian civilians killed in the last year
        When is too early to decorate for autumn?
        National Guard called out to end Lakota ceremonies
            surrounding pipeline protest
But disbelief, sadness, and anger build,
and then are assuaged by working with animals at the rehab center
and penning letters to Congress.
Tomorrow it begins again.

SPIDER PEOPLE

Eight-leggeds creep across vacuumed floors,
up paneled walls, into coffee mugs.
Screams, flying shoes halt their adventures,
send them scurrying into darkened corners.

A young burn victim enters a Quick Mart
creasing his disfigured face with a smile,
anticipating a grape snow cone.
Avoidant glances erase the smile,
forcing him out the door without his frozen treat.

A wrinkled and stooped old man
mumbles his way down the sidewalk.
Words of pity and turning heads
drive him deeper into his detached world.

Two children push their obese mother's wheelchair
across a street to the steepled building.
Bursts of laughter bow their heads,
covering them in benedictions of embarrassment.

Empathy can smooth over differences,
like a trowel across wet cement,
sooth damaged feelings,
level the playing field, and
release tears of joy.

MOTHERHOOD

She lays her eggs in a shallow hole
bordering the driveway.
At my approach, she screams loudly
running in circles on match stick legs.
To draw me further away, mama Killdeer
flops on the ground, feigning a broken wing.

The perfect day-at-the-park sunshine
clouds over with a blue-black
rain-heavy sky.
The young mother wraps her jacket
around her toddler as drops begin
and dashes to the car.

While pulling weeds
I unearth a spider
cradling her cotton-white egg sack.
Her body tenses
yet she struggles away with her unborn.
Halfway to rock safety,
she loses her grasp.
Fear freezes her movements
then survival instincts
enable her to complete the rescue.

Husband passes out on the kitchen floor
exhausted from the alcohol fueled beating
he gave her that bloodied her face
but not her resolve.
She gathers her remaining strength,
swaddles her sleeping baby,
takes a bus to the shelter.

A sea turtle lumbers
up and down the starlit beach
before selecting the perfect spot
to deposit her eggs.
Her job complete,
she returns to the sea.

Alone and homeless
her options are few for her baby
born under the viaduct.
She wraps him in newspapers
and places him on the church steps
wondering if the loss of his mother's love
will forever haunt him.

Motherhood
instincts tempered by circumstances.

LOSING MY RELIGION

It began to crumble
when the black robed nun,
her face framed in white accordion pleats,
told her first graders:
"Animals do not have souls."
She lied.
I knew my floppy-eared puppy's soul
was bigger than hers—
his was filled with love.

It became dust at
my father-in-law's Catholic funeral.
No priest's words could stop my uncontrolled tears,
not the hymns, crucifix, Bible verses,
In-the-name-of-the-Father prayers,
Nothing.
Until the sound of drums
and smell of wood smoke
lured me outside
to feel my connection to the earth.

All traces were swept away
at my former husband's funeral.
We had grown apart but never out of love.
The priest spoke of his lost 25 years
living an unholy life, married to me.
But we were not lost.
None of those Christians
in their all-or-nothing religiosity
could erase what we had together.

The voice in my soul awakens
with a cat's purr, blowing river winds,
crisp pine scent, coyote howls,
not from recited words in a steepled place.

LIFE WITHOUT PAROLE

Hope slips through fingers
like time spent waiting
often just a tick ahead,
visible, but elusive.
Or it hangs back like a stopped clock
no longer viable.

Hope survives fire, preserved
beneath blackened structures
housing every possession.
It resides beneath blankets
of the terminally ill until handfuls of dirt
hit casket lids.
It drips down the sides of chilled
liquor bottles and heroin needles
passing through moments, days, years of addiction.

Hope does not reside in a fear-frozen rabbit
before the hawk descends,
nor in dry corn stalks waiting for rain.
Hope grows within human souls.
It sets us apart, keeps us alive.

Steel doors enclose him forever.
There is no hope for a lifer.
He will spend 60 plus years
never thought to be better than his worst moment.
Kindness to fellow prisoners and guards,
knowledge gained for personal growth,
feelings of remorse and guilt for his crime
mean nothing, betterment of his situation…
impossible, given a sentence of revenge,
a life devoid of a point, a reason, a direction.
Stress and depression will dull his mind.
Lack of exercise, proper food, and sleep
will shrivel his body.
And the absence of hope will wither his soul.
A most torturous demise.

FLAG R AND R

High atop a pole the park flag
is wind-caught in a riverbank pine,
the stars and stripes unwaving,
yearning for serenity,
unfurled within scented branches.

Calm river water
flows across rocks, between fish,
and up against the shoreline.
Peaceful sunshine dries the rain soaked cloth,
greens the grass, perks wilted flowers,
casts squirrels' shadows
as they chase along the pine.

The flag flutters as a breeze
jumps from treetop to trail post
to floating geese upon shallow waters.
It stiffens
refusing to wave back
into the chaos.

FOG RUNNING

Desire to capture its softness
wrap it around like a blanket
and nap beneath a tree,
but fog makes the tall green ones
invisible, like female
potential in my parents' eyes.
Damn, such digressions go against—
Fog Lessons:
    Live in the moment, just the ten feet
    of visibility around me.
    Muffled car sounds seem like distant animal noises,
    covering up all vestiges of civilization
    just the cool fog dripping from my hair,
    and the clear screech of a blue jay,
    no past visible behind me,
    or future ahead of my stride.
    Just now.

ECHO MEMORIES

Another meeting at a library
a short distance from my previous life.
I escape the October wind
through automatic doors that open
right up to a silent table spread
with Pavarotti books, CD's, DVD's
honoring a man newly deceased.
Seeing his bearded face on a book cover
sets his rich familiar voice echoing
among the book shelves, computer tables,
and sounds of children reading.
His tenor the measurement of greatness.

Meeting ends, not too long this time.
I retrace my steps along computer tables
where some of the same faces still stare at screens.

Pavarotti's fullness washes away all immediacy
bouncing off books longing to be read,
clearing the mind of all that is not beautiful.
Just as he brings ears to tiptoe
by reaching high C.

But the richest voice ever heard is suddenly replaced
by blood thumping through my veins,
my pounding heart.
A policeman packing a gun
leans against a study carol,
not book browsing,
nor Internet searching,
but warding off imaginary violence.
Just a few years earlier, I took bike rides through this neighborhood
with my young daughter
to this monument to free speech.

Library—knowledge for the taking,
a sanctuary,
but now containing a weapon of death
to teach violence as a problem solving tool.

Sounds of peaceful reading and
Pavarotti beauty
echo now in memory only.

DOCUMENTARY: ROCK PERCEPTIONS

Fade-in on:
>A huge bolder,
>lichens etch a lacy pattern across the
>base, weaving over nicks and cracks
>"earned through centuries of
>life absorptions,"
>says a Samuel L. Jacksonesque rock voice.

Pan to a:
>9/11 blue sky,
>follow a distant black dot looming larger,
>forming into an eagle, talons ready to
>pounce—
>crouching cottontail safe
>within rock's shadow.
>Another aerial visitor glides to the
>hard surface, resting
>weary wings.
>A multi-hued hissing cockroach
>leans against its hardness
>contemplating the future.
>"All their soul energy
>seeps into my hard surface giving
>me breath, peace, and knowledge."

Close-up of:
>Moccasined feet stepping on by
>as if valued crops were beneath,
>footprints nonexistent.
>Tobacco offering flying across his hardness.
>Words of rock medicine thanksgiving
>echo over the hills.

Wide shot of:
>Prairie below,
>sun kissed tall grasses lean eastward
>blown by powerful west winds.
>Soldiers lock step up and over the hills.

Fade-in on:
> Furrowed faces intent upon
> killing those who came before,
> taking possession of their lands.
> Their evil energy
> blocks the sun's rays
> turns red, orange, and yellow flower
> petals to gray-browns.
> Grass crushed under dead weight,
> bloody fingers
> block airways,
> "I cannot breathe."

Wide angle on:
> Slow motion clouds kaleidoscoping their way across
> the sky
> in wave
> > after wave
> > > after wave.

Medium shot of:
> Young woman rock perched
> writing inspired thoughts in
> a flowered notebook.
> Feeling rock energy,
> passion, knowledge, and all it has
> Survived.

ESCAPE

She hides in her colored pencil box,
shading her loneliness in protective lavender.
Once fully obscured, she emerges ready to treat her ears
to nature sounds along the river's edge.
Brisk current cascades over flat boulders,
mimicking the occasional splashes of fish jumps.
Gulls cry out, announcing their successes at finding food.
A rarely seen otter takes a shoreline swim,
making almost imperceptible ripples.
Her quiet gazing allows a chipmunk to sit just inches away,
washing his paws and face, post meal.
As a couple holding hands walks by,
she tries to clutch her protective lavender.
It begins to fade, so she hurries home to
her colors and the comforting purr of her cat.

JUST THE WAY IT IS

A colorful autumn
sunset radiates through
my windshield as
his van swaggers down the road
ahead of me
spraying pride mixed with
droplets of blood
dripping down a bumper shelf
attached to the back end.
Strapped to it
a deer
no longer running through forests
spraying joyful deer spirit.

High in a tree stand, the
hunter may have spent hours eating
sandwiches, drinking thermos coffee
and waiting—
for a buck with bragging rights antlers.
His tree top assault
required no training, no skills,
no mental acuity,
just a high powered telescoped gun,
yet will no doubt provide months of
retelling, barroom, beer swilling
joy—
as if this air attack upon the
defenseless was a true test of his
testosterone level.

The deer hearse inches up
his steep
home on the river driveway,
care taken not to spill his
quarry on the asphalt.

Immersed in his story, I pause to observe
him exiting the van, his grinning,
pride bloated form
careens up the sidewalk
like a pinball.

"I bagged one!" he shouts with all the
braggadocio of a
victorious gladiator, ecstatic
over his conquest.
With hunters,
that's just the way it is.

PLOT TWIST

Facebook is nothing but unedited movie scenes
most meant for the cutting room floor
visible in bold colors
like shots of
over-sized ice cream sundaes,
calorie laden burgers and fries.

Actors vie for Oscar status
requesting confidence-boosting "likes"
and praise for turning another year older.

The plot, "Hey! Look at me," plays out
in vacation stills around the Eiffel Tower,
on San Marcos beaches,
and in one-year-ago-remembrance scenes
of new cars, honor roll grandchildren, and cats wearing hats.

Spliced between river cruises,
heaping plates of food,
the plot twists into violence and struggle—
a father running from bombs clutching his dead child,
hunger-lined faces of old and young in a refugee camp,
news clips of suicide bombings,
gang wars, police brutality.

Another plot twist of compassion and mindfulness
could end the movie, set the stage
for a better sequel.

NEW PATHS

Silence takes us beneath a berry bush
to view field mice sleeping with milk-filled tummies.
It surrounds a barn owl diving toward prey,
grabbing a toad before it hears a sound.
It muffles giggles, prolonging a game of Hide-and-Go-Seek
way past the street-light-coming-on curfew.
Silence uncovers our ears, letting us distinguish
sloughing wind sounds through pine trees
from shooshing leaf clapping maples.
It enables a friend to hear heartache
and offer a hug.
Silence opens our hearts to a man in a reflective vest
peddling a three-wheeled bike,
letting us feel his pride of independence.
It quiets early morning air,
revealing scratching sounds of scrabbling raccoons
chasing around a telephone pole.
Silence takes us on new paths.

WHO?

Nondescript hair color, not like the
burnt sienna crayon used for
horses, daggers, pretty doe eyes,
just brown used for
wooden planks of an old-time outhouse,
cardboard boxes flattened
and stacked for recycling.
My average height matches my
average intelligence, nose, and eyes,
and unremembered average name.
My gray car blends into
the gray asphalt, Midwestern sky,
and ground fog
as it creeps along bathed in blinding
white light from other's high beams,
I'm unseen.
I tiptoe across the earth using up
my share of fossil fuels and precious water,
depositing a fair amount into landfills.
Yes, I am here, leaving a footprint
that no one will
acknowledge, revere, or condemn.

THE PHOTO

Stop whispering about our past,
you metal framed photo,
with us decked out in wide collared shirts,
bell bottoms, and long
free-flowing hair.
Smiles holding the key to youthful innocence
or ignorance of his
hurtful wasting away mid-fifties
death.
Stop reminding me that youth was
pain free, carefree, drenched
in pansy petals that did not
freeze in winter's deadly cold,
or become ugly with
burning sunrays
and brown falling petals.
Those smiles held the future and past
in the present,
reaching for everything,
afraid of nothing,
secure in now-love.
Stop reminding me of all that is lost
in death's growth-halting grip.

LESS WORRY

Worry rides on random air particles
impossible not to ingest.
Once inside, it grows, feeding on what has meaning,
often overtaking logic.

Enjoyment of a good meal,
a page turning book, a swim in a pool
are clouded with worries for those who
live without enough food, water, ability to read.
An amusement park trip elicits thoughts of
Garbage-filled landfills and paved-over meadow lands,
spoilage for future generations.
Images of slaughterhouses and caged chickens
accompany grocery store visits.

But now, worrying about a chipmunk
living in the tree line at our road's end, can cease.
I always slowed down thirty feet from the stop sign,
anticipating his little brown striped self
scurrying across the road.
I gave him a C- for car awareness.
Today I stopped the car, picked up his little corpse,
stroked his soft tummy, released his spirit,
and laid him on soft grass beneath a tree.

Perhaps with one less worry, and
by breathing in starlight, falling leaves,
my grandsons' laughter,
hope for tomorrow can grow.

HELD IN MEMORY BY NO ONE

His last words to her as soldiers opened fire
then burned their village to the ground,
embraced her, warded off fear,
provided solace, for each remaining
moment of her life.

Pet names echoed off empty nest walls
as a retired couple peeled back memories
playing romantic games
recalled from college days.
Until they passed on
to whatever is next.

A buckeye nestled in the glove box of an old woman's car
reflected a special bond
created in secret meetings beneath that far reaching tree.
Cultivated through years of
punishing winds and energizing sunshine.
Its meaning lost with her passing.

Death erases memories
like ocean waves covering
gems buried beneath the sand.
At rest like the hearts that held them.

SKIPPING SUMMER

Smells of gunpowder from July Fourth fireworks
mix with honeysuckle, wet earth, and freshly caught fish.
She race-walks along the riverside
hoping nature can tame the painful remembrances
surrounding her least favorite season.
Years have passed since that phone call
crushed her soul.

The sun sweat-soaks her blouse
so she slows her pace trying to avoid
comparing the heat to that of four years ago
when the sky was the same shade of cloudless blue
and the grass turned brown from lack of rain.

She stops to absorb the beauty of a buckeye tree that has
surpassed summer altogether,
leaves turning red, orange, yellow.
She longs to do that— skip the season,
sidestep the anniversary of her son's murder,
travel from tulips and budding trees,
right into crisp air, crunching leaves.
Bypass all summers so she could attend
his wedding instead of his funeral,
so his sense of humor and generous spirit
could be wrapped in her arms,
not spilled on the sidewalk
during a pocket change robbery.

She picks a buckeye pod from the ancient tree,
hoping it will cover over the remembering,
keep her boy forever safe in her heart.

I MADE IT OUT

My head is tilted skyward with the pride of it all.
warm sunshine not blocked by city buildings
caresses my cheeks.
An uncontrollable smile is brightened by
autumn colored maple trees
lining the smooth sidewalk.
No dodging of broken bottles, trash, and gunshot
induced blood spatters required
as I glide my son's
stroller to the park.

I made it out.
No more meals at the center
to save tuition money or 2AM walks
home from serving drinks and
fending off drunken aggressions.

His giggles reverberate off the
wooden playground structures as
I guide him down the slippery slide,
his soft black curls blowing in the breeze.

Other mothers blurt out
"oohs" and "awws"
watching him toddle over to the sandbox and
plop down next to his little blonde-haired friend.

I relish this,
hoping as he ages that the
baby "aww" moments won't be replaced
by black man fear.
Perhaps by then
color won't matter.

FADING FIRE

Mantel photos of unfamiliar faces peer into her
clouded over mind.
The crackling fire and smell of wood smoke shift her gaze,
unveiling memories of being a young mother,
hanging stockings from that mantel, making Christmas cookies,
joining her children and husband in off-key caroling.
A rush of cold air brings her back to the strange room, its
unknown people.

The words needed to question where and who
have long since blended with the smoke,
risen into the night sky.
Soon the logs will cease to hold a flame.

ALL THE WORLD'S A STAGE

Some believe all is predetermined,
we but actors playing out a script.
Perhaps…
But the director has gone out for coffee
or is planet hopping in another galaxy,
for we are certainly on our own.

The script states thou shalt not kill.
So who is directing our drones
of hatred that murder and maim,
giving the stage direction,
find your mark, a catastrophic meaning?

The script states thou shalt not steal.
Shouldn't the director step in
as the action is up-staged by
big oil claiming eminent domain
for their profits?
And special interests stealing elections?

Who is directing this play?
Who is making sure the actors
give as much as they take from one another
as they work toward the whole
benefitting all upon earth's stage?
Nobody.
The director has left the building,
if indeed he was ever present.

MANAGING RHYTHMS

Earth's rhythms placate her soul
as Bach cantatas cool her brow
against jagged beats pulsing
from harsh clanging sounds of hatred,
generating a rapid cadence,
a metronome in gale force winds.

Her rhythm, a discordant beat
beneath her hijab,
tries to escape comments hurled
at her religion, culture, essence
through media and personal affronts,
and move back into tones smoothed
by snow falling on chickadee heads
clustered around her backyard feeder.
Her home a family sanctuary
pulsing in tune with earth equanimity.

Like an ear-piercing scream
racist words scrawl across her garage door,
shattering the calm, sending ragged fear rhythms
deep within her soul.
She feels the hatred.

Outrage explodes throughout the community.
Circling the curse words with a large pink heart,
they stand in her driveway,
carrying signs calling for peace,
while the symphony plays Bach,
and a new door is donated.

Her earth rhythm returns,
charged with pulses of compassion.

MOON MEDITATION

The moon eases above the horizon,
silvering autumn leaves,
painting a golden path across the pond.
Her light never judges, illuminating all
in unfractured reflections of beauty.
A young woman luxuriates in the moon's glow,
covering her body in yellow beams of that which is,
void of right or wrong, good or bad, less or more.
Her skin absorbs the moon's reality, lacking
interpretation, enlightening her soul with compassion.
She can now face the harshness often reflected by others.

ONE

This hand, claw, wing, hoof, paw, fist …
present, past, future, now—
the same—
One.
Knowing this One, enlightens,
connects all to all, up to down,
always.
Sounds good, but does it
translate?
At One with the guy who cuts you
      off in traffic?
At One with the serial killer, rapist, child
      molester, animal abuser, warmonger?
My paw cannot hold up the world
      against destructive Ones.
So suspend judgment, join paws to stars,
      connect and Be.
Easy—cell to cell, hand to claw, to wing,
      to hoof, to paw, to fist, to
All.

CULTURAL FABRIC

Cartoon images adorn numbered squares of calendars,
reflecting the warp of our cultural fabric.
We celebrate most with three-day weekends, store-wide sales,
over-indulgent food consumption,
and twisted myths.

We drink green beer in our green clothes, one day in March,
mimicking a culture of immigrants
we once considered worthless drunks.

School children make stone soup, wear paper Pilgrim hats,
and feathered headbands, celebrating
a Thanksgiving that never happened,
fictional dinner created to mask a genocide.

We honor laborers in September
with parades, weekend sales,
a day off without pay,
as they struggle to make ends meet.

Religious holidays, created to counter pagan ceremonials,
have left churches, entering shopping malls,
fueling the race toward consumption,
where he who dies with the most stuff wins.

Our cultural weft weaves over and under the greenbacks
with threads of compassion, self-sacrifice, and hope.

That same calendar reflects love for mothers and fathers,
a giving spirit in that big red kettle in December,
and honor in January for a man who died trying to free his people.

This is who we are,
the face staring back in the mirror,
brought to our attention every month.

RUTH

She's seated cross-legged on a flat-top rock,
bathed in cool pre-dawn air,
unable to sleep, her mind on fast forward.

Another successful camping trip underway.
Her best friends with guy-of-the-moment
—hers is long gone—
sleeping off last night's drinking games.

Dew enhances autumn leaf colors,
oranges, reds, yellows waving
in western breezes at sunrise.

She contemplates the hours ahead
kayaking, playing Frisbee golf, hiking, campfire cooking,
every moment carefully planned,
free time as scarce as lasting love.

Her Down syndrome fetus begins to flutter.
Options cycle over and over through her mind
on a spinning wheel of misfortune:
    Keep him.
    Eliminate him.
    Send him away.

Ruth, queen of organization,
master of goal achievement,
faces a crossroads, lacking
even an inkling of the correct direction.

As the sun warms them, his kicks
bring a smile to her face,
a protective hand upon her stomach.

Karen Wolf has an undergraduate degree in Education from the University of Toledo and a Master of Arts degree from Bowling Green State University. She taught English for 30 years, enjoying the challenges and breakthroughs of dealing with high school students. Teaching also afforded her time to spend with her daughter, Addie, sharing breaks and summers off.

Karen then opened her own pet sitting company. Her passion for animals enabled her to grow the business to 70 clients. After 12 years of working seven days a week and every holiday, it was time to semi-retire and spend more time with her grandsons, Presley and Tate.

She also volunteers at Nature's Nursery Wildlife Rehabilitation Center. She cares for 35 permanent residents who are used as education ambassadors because they cannot be released. And she brings injured and orphaned animals to the center for care and eventual release.

Poetry has been a constant in Karen's life ever since she penciled her first poem in first grade bemoaning the death of grass each winter. She says that poetry soothes the savage beast and opens her eyes to the beauty that abounds within the world.

www.ingramcontent.com/pod-product-compliance
Lightning Source LLC
LaVergne TN
LVHW041557070426
835507LV00011B/1148